D0478657

Otters

by **Wil Mara**

Marshall Cavendish
Benchmark
New York

Marshall Cavendish Benchmark
99 White Plains Road
Tarrytown, New York 10591-9001
www.marshallcavendish.us

Library of Congress Cataloging-in-Publication Data

Mara, Wil.
Otters / by Wil Mara.
p. cm. — (Animals, animals)
Summary: "Describes the physical characteristics, habitat, behavior, diet,
life cycle, amd conservation status of the otter"—Provided by publisher.
Includes bibliographical references and index.
ISBN-13: 978-0-7614-2527-4
1. Otters—Juvenile literature. I. Title.
QL737.C25M283 2007
599.769—dc22
2006020823

Photo research by Candlepants Incorporated

Cover photo: Kennan Ward/Corbis

The photographs in this book are used by permission and through the courtesy of:
Super Stock: age fotostock, 1, 14. *Corbis:* Roger De La Harper; Gallo Images, 4; Bettman, 34; Jonathon Blair, 38;
Natalie Fobes, 40; Kennan Ward, 42. *Minden Pictures:* Frans Lanting, 6, 15, 27, 28, 26, 42; Ingo Arndt/Foto Natura, 11;
Gerry Ellis, 19; Claus Meyer, 21; Gerry Ellis/Globio, 23; Norbert Wu, 24; Tim Fitzharris, 30. *Peter Arnold Inc.:*
Fred Bruemmer, 9; Nicole Duplaix, 12; Gerald Lacz, 32; ullstein-blw Naturstudio, 33; Malcolm Schuyl, 36.
Getty Images: John Warden, 22; Johnny Johnson, 39.

Printed in Malaysia
6 5 4 3 2

Contents

Meet the Otter

Otters seem to have an endless supply of energy. They spend hours playing both in the water and on land. They are also skilled hunters and, in the case of the females, strong and protective parents. As *carnivores*, otters include other animals as part of their diet. Otters are found throughout much of the world, although they are slowly disappearing in some areas.

There are about eighteen different *species*, or types, of otters. They are found on every continent except for Antarctica and Australia. The three most common species are the North American river otter, the European river otter, and the sea otter. The North American river otter is found throughout most of

Otters are among the world's most playful and energetic animals.

Did You Know . . .
The giant otter is probably the rarest of all otter species. It is found only in select areas from Venezuela to Argentina. It can grow to a length of more than 5 feet (1.5 meters) and weigh more than 70 pounds (31.7 kilograms). Experts believe there may be no more than one thousand left in the wild.

Otters always live close to water, whether it is in the form of a lake, a river, or an ocean. This one is running along a river bank in Brazil.

North America, from Alaska and Canada in the north to the southern tip of Florida. The European river otter is found, as its name suggests, across Europe, as well as in parts of

6

Asia and North Africa. The sea otter is found from the coasts of Japan and the Kamchatka Peninsula in Asia, throughout the Pacific Ocean to the western coasts of

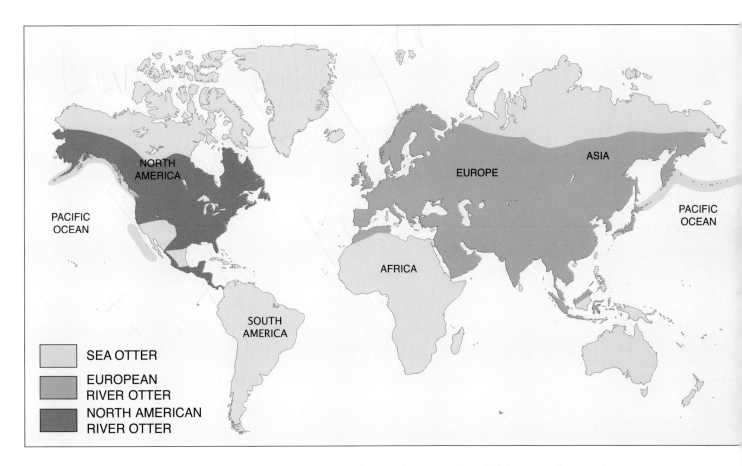

Otters are found on every continent except Australia and Antarctica. This map shows that otters have not settled in the extreme north and south, where it is too cold for them to survive.

Species Chart

Length (body): 25 to 35 inches
(63.5 to 89 centimeters)

Length (tail): 12 to 18 inches
(30.5 to 46 centimeters)

Weight: 10 to 30 pounds (4.5 to 13.5 kilograms)

Height (ground to shoulder): 10 to 14 inches
(25.5 to 35.5 centimeters)

Coloration: Chestnut brown in river otters, darker brown and often with gray or silver tips in marine (ocean-living) species. Lighter coloring is common on the underside of the necks and the bellies, sometimes almost white. Older otters usually have more silver and white fur, particularly on their heads and necks.

Life Span: 10 to 20 years, depending on the species

the United States and Canada. Most of the other otter species live in smaller places, and in some areas they are rare.

Otters always live in and around water. This is the *habitat* they prefer. Some species are at home only in the *salt water* of the oceans. Others are found only in

An otter's fur traps thousands of tiny air bubbles, which keep the animal warm and help it stay afloat.

freshwater places such as rivers, streams, lakes, and ponds. There are also a few that seek out *brackish* water, which is a mixture of both fresh and salt water. No matter where otters are found, though, when you see one, you can be sure there is water nearby.

Otters are long and slender, and are able to twist their bodies as if they were made of rubber. Their heads are wide and flat, with short ears and small, round, dark eyes. Otter noses are usually triangular or diamond shaped, with rounded corners. They have whiskers on either side that point downward and measure about 4 inches (10 centimeters) in length. Their legs are short and have tiny paws that are usually webbed. This helps make otters such skilled swimmers. Sharp, powerful claws are also common in almost every otter species. An otter's tail is usually about half as long as its body. It is an inch or two wide at the rump, then thins to a point at the end. An otter's teeth are strong, and the skin inside the mouth is especially tough.

An otter's fur is made up of two parts—an inner layer and an outer layer. The inner layer, also called the *underfur*, has millions of tiny hairs. They trap air against the otter's skin to help keep it warm and allow

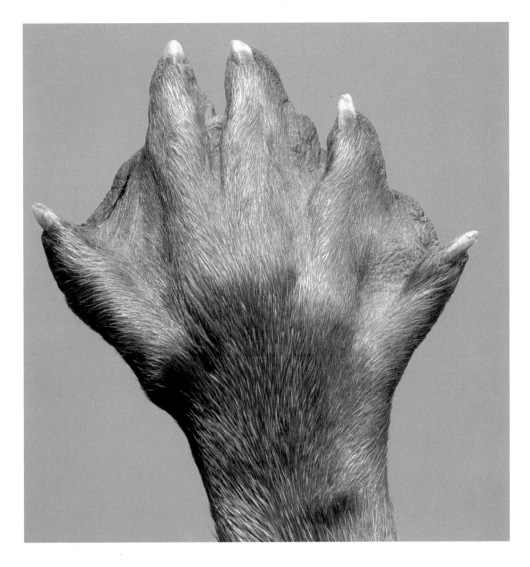

An otter's legs are short but powerful. Its paws are also webbed, which helps it swim faster.

it to float in the water. The outer layer, also called a "top coat," is made up of long, tough *guard hairs*. They protect the inner layer by helping to trap heat and keep water off the otter's delicate skin.

2 How Otters Live

Most otters are *diurnal*. That means they are active during the day and sleep at night. However, there are a few species that do the opposite—rest during the day and move about at night. The word to describe these animals is *nocturnal*. Otters that live in the ocean tend to be more active during the day. Otters that live in rivers and lakes are often active at night. One reason for this is that there are more *predators*—animals that hunt otters for food—around rivers and lakes, so it is safer for river otters to hunt at night.

Otters spend a lot of their time in search of food. Most of their favorite meals come from the water

An otter eats up to one-fifth of its total body weight every day, so it spends a lot of time searching for food. It does most of its hunting in the water, but it will prowl the shoreline from time to time.

Otters are carnivores, meaning they eat meat and thus other animals to survive. This one has caught a trout.

including fish, clams, eels, crabs, crayfish, mussels, and sea urchins. Sea urchins live on the ocean floor and look like spiny balls. An otter will dive down and scoop one up with its claws. It then swims back to the surface, where it floats on its back and uses its chest as a kind of table to hold the sea urchin while it eats.

To get into the hard shell of a clam or mussel, an otter picks up a rock, places it on its chest, then beats the shell against the rock until it breaks open. Otters that live in lakes or rivers eat other animals as well, including frogs, birds, and small mammals such as mice and voles. An otter needs to eat quite a bit, too— up to one-fifth of its body weight every day.

When otters are finished eating, they clean every spare bit of food from their fur. It is important for them to keep their fur clean. By constantly rubbing

Favorite otter foods include fish, clams, crabs, and the creature this one has caught— a sea urchin.

The Otter:

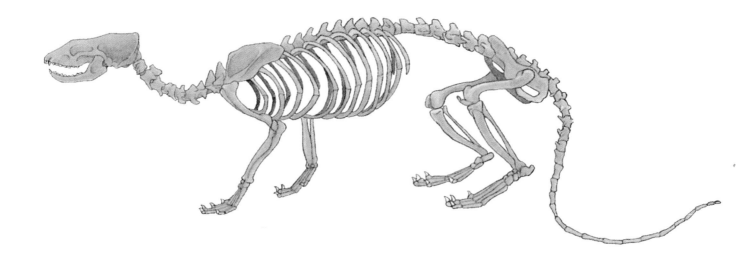

The otter is slender, with a long neck and spine. . . .

Inside and Out

Its sleek body is also very flexible, allowing the otter to bend and move in many directions.

their fur, they trap air bubbles under the fur and against their skin. These bubbles help form a layer that keeps cold water from reaching the otters' skin. Otters spend hours each day cleaning their fur with their paws and tongues. This activity also allows more air to be trapped in the underfur, which keeps the otters warmer.

Otters that live in the ocean may spend their entire lives in the water. They can be seen floating on their backs or drifting on top of *kelp* leaves. Kelp, also called seaweed, is a long algae that grows from the shallow sea floor or near large rocks. It can reach 65 feet (20 meters) or more in length. Its brownish green leaves float on the surface because they seek out sunlight. Ocean-living otters love kelp beds because they offer a place to play, hide, and rest, as well as search for food.

Otters that live in bodies of freshwater will come onto land from time to time. Even then, however, they rarely stray far from their watery homes. Some otters rest in *dens*, which they enter through underwater holes.

Otters usually hunt alone, but some species live in groups that protect one another when

Beds of kelp offer otters a safe hiding spot where they can play, rest, and hunt. Kelp is an algae that grows on rocks or on the sea floor.

danger is near. They warn one another through different sounds, such as growls, chirps, squeals, and screeches. They are also quick to jump into the water at the first sign of trouble. They are excellent swimmers, and some species can stay underwater for six to eight minutes at a time.

When otters are not resting, avoiding predators, or searching for food, they are often seen playing. As with everything else, they do most of their playing in the water. Two otters may wrestle each other, turning somersaults while harmlessly biting or kicking at their playmate. Otters have also been seen sliding down muddy or icy banks and flying into the air before

Otters float together in large groups called rafts. This behavior is most common in sea otters, which usually gather in groups of about ten to twenty.

Otters have learned that they are safer in groups than by themselves. If danger is near, one otter may warn the others through a series of vocal sounds.

diving into the water. Sometimes otters float around in large groups called *rafts*. There are usually ten to twenty otters to a raft, but there can be as many as a hundred.

The fact that otters spend so much time in groups rather than alone is one important reason they are able to survive in the wild. Just as they play together, they are also quick to warn one another when danger is near. Sticking together helps them stay alive and healthy.

3 An Otter's Life Cycle

Otters mate at different times of the year, depending on where they live. Those found in colder areas often wait until late spring or early summer. Otters living in warmer areas may mate at any point during the year. Mating season is the only time when male and female otters pay much attention to one another. This is also the only time when otters fight. A male that has found a potential female partner will chase other males away. This rarely ends in a true battle, with biting and clawing. Usually the other males give up quickly and move off to find different females. The males and females that eventually mate may live together as a family for years.

Otters come together to mate at different times of the year, depending on how warm or cold it is in the area in which they live. In warm regions, they can mate at any time.

A female otter's nose may sometimes appear pink after mating. This is because the mating process is often rough, with both the male and female getting a few cuts and scrapes.

It takes only two months for a baby otter to fully develop inside its mother. But the mother's body can do an amazing thing. It can delay, or hold off, this growth for a while so that the babies will be born at the right time of the year. This ideal time is usually when there is the most food around and that could be as much as ten months after the mother mates with the male. A mother otter also has to be healthy in order to give birth and take care of her young, so she needs plenty of food as well.

A newborn otter is called a *pup* or a *cub*. Otters that live in the ocean usually have just one pup. It is sometimes born right in the water. Other species have a *litter* of up to five or six. A normal litter, however, is two or three for most species. Species that live in the ocean, however, sometimes skip a year and have a pup every two years instead.

Sea otter pups are lighter in color and look fuzzier than their parents. They weigh about 3 to 5 pounds (1.3 to 2.2 kilograms) and are around 12 to 18 inches (30.5 to 45 centimeters) in length. They are helpless in every way—they cannot hunt, swim, or defend themselves. The mother nurses them for about

Sea otter mothers may hide their young by wrapping them in kelp leaves before diving underwater to search for food.

the first six to twelve months of their lives. She finds food for them and keeps them clean. She also protects them, which can be her most important role of all. A mother sea otter, for example, will place her pup on her chest while swimming on her back. She leaves it only when she has to dive in search of food. River otters, on the other hand, usually leave their pups inside their *dens.*

A newborn otter pup lives off its mother's milk. The pups of some species will also start eating solid

Mother otters take excellent care of their young. They clean them, teach them how to swim, and find food for them. Some otter babies are able to eat solid food after just a few weeks.

It is important for otters to keep their fur clean at all times. If it gets too dirty, it will not trap enough air bubbles underneath, and the otter may freeze in the chilly water. This mother is cleaning her pup until it is able to do so on its own.

Otter mothers give their offspring "swimming lessons." First they let them float, then they watch as the young learn to paddle around. Pups are ready to be on their own in less than a year.

foods after only a few weeks. The mother teaches the babies how to swim, search for food, and clean its fur. During a swimming lesson, a mother otter lets go of her newborn and allows it to float, hoping the little one will use its natural *instincts* to figure out how to paddle through the water. But the mother always remains close by. Some otter pups may be ready to live on their own after about six to eight months. Young sea otters can start their own families after just three or four years. They may move as far as 40 to 50 miles (64 to 80.5 kilometers) from where they were raised.

4 Survival in the Wild

Otters don't have many predators, but they do have a few. Otters living in rivers and lakes have to beware of jaguars, bobcats, and other big cats. Other predators they must watch out for include wolves, foxes, bears, and alligators and crocodiles. While not a direct threat, large birds such as hawks and eagles are also known to steal food from otters, especially at times when it is scarce.

Otters that live in the ocean enjoy a fairly peaceful life, with almost no predators. In recent years, however, killer whales have begun eating otters by the

Various big cats, such as this ocelot, are among the few animals that prey on otters. Other predators include wolves and foxes. But they have to be quick. Otters are smart and always stay close to water.

thousands. Part of the reason for this change is that many of the other animals that killer whales once relied on for food have vanished. This lack of prey forces them to eat whatever they can find.

Humans are a great threat to otters as well. Hundreds of years ago, the meat from one otter would be used to feed a small family for a day or two, and the fur could be made into items of clothing. The fur from an otter is called a *pelt*. It was prized because it did such a good job of holding in body heat. The fur also sheds water. A coat made from otter pelts could protect people from the worst winter storms. Pelts

Killer whales were not always otter predators, but they are now. In some areas, these giant mammals cannot find the foods they prefer, such as seals. So they are forced to seek out other animals as a source of food.

The main reason so many otters have been killed by humans is because of their fur. It is sleek and sheds water well.

could be made into warm blankets and other items as well. Otter pelts are also strong and stay in good condition for a long time.

Early humans hunted other animals as well, so at first otters were not *endangered*. That changed in the 1700s when thousands of men traveling in ships from Asia and Europe discovered otters by the millions along the

Did You Know . . .

Some experts believe sea otters are occasionally eaten by sharks that think they are seals instead. In some cases the sharks may then spit out the otters, which do not always survive the accidental attack.

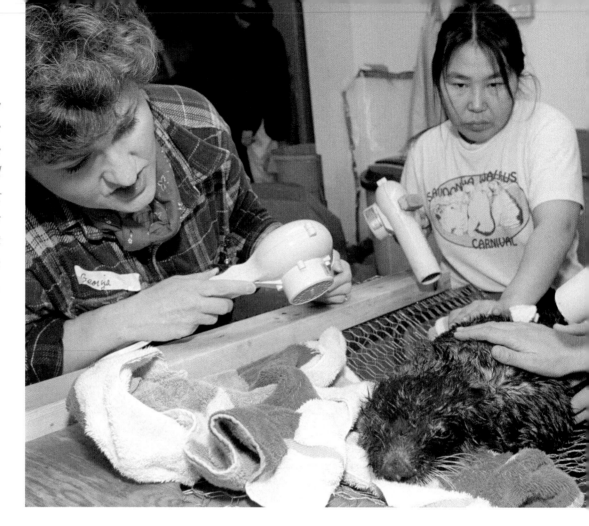

There are now thousands of people worldwide who have given their time and energy to protecting otters. Here, workers clean an otter that has been the victim of an oil spill.

various coastlines they visited and explored. They killed the otters for food and clothing. Later they brought otter pelts back to their home countries and soon realized that each fur fetched a high price. From then on, people sought out otters for no other reason than to catch and sell their pelts for a profit. Millions of otters were hunted and killed for this reason.

In the early 1900s, several nations got together and created laws to protect otters. As a result, populations had a chance to grow again. However, there are still problems caused by people to this day. Oil spills in areas where sea otters live usually kill hundreds, if not thousands, at a time. These accidents happen when a large ship carrying millions of gallons of oil comes too close to the shore and hits ground. This can tear a hole in the ship's bottom or side, causing the oil to spill out. The oil then sticks to the otters' fur. As a result, the otters cannot trap air underneath their fur, and often they freeze to death. If they try licking off the oil, they die from swallowing it.

Otters that live in streams and lakes often become sick due to *pesticides* and other chemicals that are dumped into the water or sprayed in forests. People who fish for a living also sometimes catch so many crabs, clams, and other seafood in their nets that the sea otters end up with little to eat. These foods that otters depend on for their survival are also removed or destroyed through dredging (making a waterway deeper), trapping, or they are collected and sold to pet stores.

5 The Future of the Otter

The fate of otters around the world is uncertain. In some places, there are thriving groups that were once at the risk of disappearing. In other places, populations continue to get smaller. People still pose a great threat to the otter's future. As towns and neighborhoods grow and spread, more and more land is claimed to build places such as homes and factories. Accidents like oil spills or forest fires only make matters worse. When an otter habitat is destroyed, the otters are unable to find enough of the food they need to survive.

Some animals become *extinct*, which means they disappear from the planet entirely. Most animals that

Only through the hard work of concerned people and organizations will otters be ensured a bright future.

Otters that have lost their parents are often brought into captivity for their own safety. They are fed and kept in a clean place until they are old enough to be put back into the wild.

are at risk of extinction are now protected by laws and by organizations that care about the future and welfare of animals. One such organization is known as *CITES*. These five letters stand for the Convention on the International Trade in Endangered Species of Wild Flora and Fauna. Many nations around the world belong to CITES. It has created laws that protect rare plants and animals from extinction. Almost

Another way to protect otters living in an unsafe place is to move them to a different location. The hope is that the otters will breed in their new home and that their colony will begin to grow quickly.

all otter species are now on CITES's list, which means they cannot be sold or traded among member countries. Still it is hard to stop some people from trapping otters. Just as difficult is making sure the laws designed to protect otters are being obeyed.

Sometimes otters are removed from dangerous places in the wild and placed in captive breeding programs. The otters are usually taken to zoos or other places where they will be safe.

Another problem that otters face is habitat destruction. People sometimes harm or destroy an area where a *colony* of otters is living in order to develop land for human use. As people take up more room, otters and the other animals that live near these growing communities and neighborhoods lose that space.

On a more positive note, some otters have a remarkable ability to *repopulate*. They produce babies quickly, creating stronger and healthier colonies. Scientists have started new otter colonies in areas where they felt the otters could best survive. If, for example, an otter habitat is in danger of being destroyed because a new shopping mall is being built, scientists can trap all of the otters living in that area. They can then move the otters to a new and safer location.

Also, there are otter experts who now run *captive breeding programs.* If a group of otters has lost members, a few adults are taken from the wild and kept in a safe place, such as a zoo. The otters are fed the best food, kept clean, and given plenty of room in which to play in the hope that they will eventually

Did You Know . . .

Otters have a homing instinct similar to that of cats, dogs, and many other *mammals.* Otters that have been moved from one habitat to another have found their way back to their original home, even if it was many miles away.

41

Like other creatures living in the wild, otters do best when they—and their habitats—are left alone. The more people interfere with the delicate balance of nature, the more problems will likely be caused.

mate. When they do, and once the babies are old enough to leave their mothers, the young otters may be returned to the wild, and a new healthy generation joins an existing colony or starts a new one of its own. This plan will only work, however, if the otters are put in a habitat that is safe and provides plenty of food.

Perhaps the most important thing we can do to help otters, both now and in the future, is to leave them and their habitats alone. Because otters are not hunted or trapped as much as they used to be, otter populations are growing again in many places. In other areas, however, otters are treated as pests. There are some species that are moving ever closer to extinction. More work needs to be done to stop that from happening and to make sure these playful creatures always have a place on earth.

Glossary

brackish—Slightly salty; used to describe a mixture of sea water and freshwater.

captive breeding program—A program designed to have animals mate and give birth in captivity, where the young can then grow and develop safely.

carnivore—An animal that eats other animals.

CITES—An organization aimed at stopping the global trade of endangered plants and animals. Many nations take part in CITES.

colony—A group of animals living and thriving in a certain area.

cub—A baby otter.

den—An underground home for otters, usually found along the shores of a body of water.

diurnal—Active during the daytime.

endangered—An animal whose population has shrunk so much there is the threat that it might become extinct.

extinct—Killed off, no longer in existence.

freshwater—Any body of water containing little or no salt.

guard hairs—The hairs that make up the outer layer of fur on an otter.

habitat—The place in the wild where an animal lives.

instinct—An ability or behavior that an animal is born with.

kelp—Sea algae with long leaves that usually grow into thick underwater gardens, giving sea otters a good hiding place.

litter—A group of baby otters.

mammal—Any warm-blooded animal covered in body hair and having a mother that produces milk to feed its young.

nocturnal—Active at night.

pelt—The fur-covered skin that has been removed from an otter's body.

pesticide—A chemical used to kill insects and other small animals thought to be "pests."

predator—An animal that kills another for food.

pup—A baby otter.

raft—A group of otters floating together.

repopulate—To increase in number; to place animals into the wild so a colony can begin growing again.

salt water—Water with a high salt content, such as ocean water.

species—A group of animals that has the same physical traits and that can mate and produce similar offspring.

underfur—The inner layer of fur on an otter's body, made of millions of tiny hairs. It traps air in bubbles, keeping the otter warm and helping it stay afloat.

Find Out More

Books

Hirschmann, Kris. *Sea Otters.* Detroit: KidHaven Press, 2005.

Lockwood, Sophie. *Sea Otters.* Chanhassen, MN: Child's World, 2006.

Ransford, Sandy. *Otter.* Boston: Kingfisher, 2003.

Ring, Susan. *Project Otter.* New York: Weigl Publishers, 2003.

Tregarthen, J. C. *The Life Story of an Otter.* Cornwall, England: Cornwall Editions Limited, 2005.

VanBlaricom, Glenn. *Sea Otters.* Stillwater, MN: Voyageur Press, 2001.

Web Sites

Animal Diversity's page on sea otters
http://animaldiversity.ummz.umich.edu/site/accounts/information/enhydra_lutris.html

Friends of the Sea Otter
http://www.seaotters.org/

Kids' Planet page on sea otters
http://www.kidsplanet.org/factsheets/otter.html

National Geographic Creature Feature: River Otters
http://www.nationalgeographic.com/kids/
    creature_feature/0006/otters.html

Wikipedia page on otters
http://en.wikipedia.org/wiki/otter

About the Author

Wil Mara has written many educational books for young readers, covering topics such as science, geography, sports, notable people, and other animals. Further information about these titles can be found at his Web site—www.wilmara.com

Index

Page numbers for illustrations are in **boldface**.